PANJAB

GOSPEL AND CULTURES PAMPHLET 5

PANJAB
The Movement of the Spirit

James Massey

WCC Publications, Geneva

Cover: The Golden Temple at Amritsar
Cover photo: Len Sirman
Cover design: Edwin Hassink/WCC

ISBN 2-8254-1177-9

© 1996 WCC Publications, World Council of Churches,
150 route de Ferney, 1211 Geneva 2, Switzerland

No. 5 in the Gospel and Cultures series

Printed in Switzerland

Table of Contents

vii INTRODUCTION: THE LAND OF THE FIVE RIVERS

1 1. THE HISTORICAL AND CULTURAL CONTEXT

8 2. THE GOSPEL AT WORK IN PANJAB

18 3. ENCOUNTER AND RESPONSES

32 4. THE CONTINUING CHALLENGE TO PANJABI CHRISTIANS

35 SELECTED BIBLIOGRAPHY

Introduction: The Land of the Five Rivers

The "Panjab" of this pamphlet is the Panjab of old, where five rivers full of water once flowed. The partition at the time of independence in 1947 divided not only Panjab but also the five rivers. Two-and-a-half rivers are left with the Indian Panjab; the rest have gone to Pakistan. But in spite of this division, the wheatlands on both sides still thrive, and the overall progress continues in the cities and villages. On both sides Panjabis are still Panjabis, so our focus here on the old, undivided Panjab is warranted.

"Panjab" — the spelling we shall use in preference to the generally Anglicized form "Punjab" — is indeed an appropriate name for this land, because the word is a compound of the Persian *panj* meaning "five" and *ab* meaning "water" or "river". The five rivers of Panjab are the Jhelum, Chenab, Ravi, Beas and Sutlej.

Older physical maps of India make clear the overall geographical composition and the natural boundaries of the area which we call Panjab. Its frontiers are marked on the northwest side by some of the highest mountains in the world — the Himalayas. To the west are the small chains of hills which separate the plains of India from the Hindu Kush. To the south, the fertile lands run into the large deserts of Rajasthan and Sindh. On the eastern side the boundary line is less clear, but normally it is taken up to the Jamuna river, near Karnal in Haryana. Seen thus, the Panjab with which we are concerned here covers almost the entire present northwest India and the Panjab of Pakistan.

The World Council of Churches' study of "Gospel and Cultures" comes at a time when many cultural communities all over the globe are struggling either to maintain or to regain their cultural identities. Whether in the name of a "New World Order" promulgated by a superpower or superpowers or, in a country like India, in the name of "national integration" or bringing everyone into one "mainstream line", serious attacks are being made which are crushing small minority communities and their cultural identities.

In fact, until recently, following the major missionary traditions, Indian theologians and Christian thinkers also limited their own efforts to present and interpret the Christian gospel by taking into consideration only the so-called majority religious or cultural traditions (classical or Brahmanical Hinduism). The result is a terrible failure in the overall mission task of the church. This particularly affects North India, which includes North-West, Northern, Central, Eastern and Western India, and which covers 73 percent of the territory of the country. In this area covering nearly three-quarters of the sub-continent, not even one-fourth of one percent of the population are Christians. Almost two-thirds of the approximately 20 million Christians of India are in the four states of South India, which covers only 21 percent of the territory. Fourteen percent of Indian Christians are in North-East India (6 percent of the territory). In the larger section of North India there are only five million Christians, of whom more than 90 percent come from Dalit background (considered by their opponents as "untouchables" and by the Indian government as "Scheduled Caste"). North-West India or the Panjab, with which we are concerned in this pamphlet, is part of this larger section of North India.

The main factor responsible for this failure on the part of both missionaries and Indian Christians has been a narrow approach which has regarded Indian culture as one composite culture. This was a serious theological and missiological mistake; and one may hope that the WCC study process on "Gospel and Cultures" can help in initiating steps towards correction.

In this pamphlet Chapter 1 will discuss briefly the historical, social and cultural context of Panjab into which the gospel came. We shall look in Chapter 2 at the functioning of the gospel as a "movement of the Spirit". In Chapter 3 some of the concrete responses to the gospel in Panjab through stories and literary illustrations will be spelled out. Chapter 4 concludes with some challenges to Panjabi Christians in the present context.

1. The Historical and Cultural Context

The history of Panjabi Christianity

Panjabi Christianity is one of the youngest Christian communities in India. It was the Presbyterians in the United States (American Presbyterian Mission), who sent the first missionary, John C. Lowrie, to Panjab. Lowrie arrived in Ludhiana on 5 November 1834 and established the first mission station in Panjab there.

There is evidence that Christianity was present in Panjab even before the arrival of Lowrie. The earliest reference to this comes from the writings of the first Sikh theologian, Bhai Gurdas (1646-1737), who wrote in one of his works known as *var* (ballad):

> *Isai* [Christians] *Musai* [Jews],
> *Haumaim* [self-centred], *Hairane* [confused].

From these few words we can deduce that there were Christians in and around Panjab during the 17th and 18th centuries, and we may possibly infer something about the kind of life these Christians were living. But it is not possible to say definitely which Christians Bhai Gurdas was referring to. We do know that around that time some Jesuit priests were living in the court of the Muslim Moghul Emperor Akbar (1556-1605). Their relationship with the Muslim religious leaders was not cordial. For example, John Clark Archer in his book on *The Sikhs* (Princeton, 1946) reports that a certain Padre Rodolph once challenged an *ulema* (Muslim scholar) to prove which of the two revelations was true, promising that if the *ulema* would carry the Quran through the fire, he would carry the Bible through it afterwards in the same way. It has also been said that Popes Gregory XIII and Clement VIII were in contact with Emperor Akbar.

Going back even further, the apocryphal book "Acts of Thomas" says that the Apostle Thomas came to Panjab during the reign of King Gundaphorus, the last Parthian ruler, in the middle of the first century. While the "Acts of Thomas" is an apocryphal document, it is also true that King

Gundaphorus was an historical figure, and some coins and a stone with an inscription of his name and date as 46 CE can be seen in the museum in Lahore, Pakistan. The historicity of King Gundaphorus has led some historians like J.N. Farquhar to suggest that St Thomas possibly travelled by sea to Panjab where he preached and converted some people. On this view, because of the invasion of Kushan, he later left Panjab via Socotra for Malabar in South India. It is also believed that converts or Christians of St Thomas were wiped out by the Kushan invasion.

However, it is virtually impossible to prove this story of St Thomas and of a Christian presence in Panjab during the first century because of the non-continuity of any Christian tradition from that time. Nor do we have any evidence which shows that the Roman Catholic priests present in Akbar's court were able to establish any church or Christian community. To all intents and purposes, therefore, the real history of Christianity in Panjab begins with the arrival of John C. Lowrie. Almost all Indian church historians have accepted this as a fact, and therefore our concern in this pamphlet is with Christianity in Panjab from 1834 to the present day.

Before moving on to discuss the cultural context, it may be useful to look at some short passages from an address given by the secretary of the American Missionary Society, Elijah P. Swift, to the first group of missionaries leaving for this part of India, including James Wilson, John Newton and Julia Davis, in October 1834. An extract from this address has been quoted in Newton's *History of A.P. Missionaries in India* (1886). Swift's comments offer some insights into the political and geographical context of the 19th century, when Christianity entered Panjab:

> It is also gratifying to know that Northern India, and especially the Seik [Sikh] Nation, the field, and the people to which you repair, present encouragements of the most inviting character... The Seiks occupy a considerable part of the province of Lahore, in the north-westerly part of Hindostan, a territory 320 miles in length and 220 in breadth; a part of Multan adjoining it

on the south-west, and part of Delhi in the south-east... The country of the Seik nation, therefore, comprises the warm alluvial and fertile plains of the Panjab, and the high and salubrious elevations of the south base of the Himalayas, to which a mission intended for the Seiks might doubtless be removed if any important advantage were likely to grow out of such an arrangement.

Newton himself is more explicit about why Panjab was favoured as a mission field, referring to the long history which serves as the background to Panjabi religious and social culture:

After much consideration they chose the Panjab. No other section is so full of historic interest as this. It was from here that Hinduism spread over the whole peninsula. It was here that the great battle was fought which is described in the Mahabharat. It was through Panjab that every successful invasion of India has taken place, except the British. It was here that the tide of Alexander's victories terminated. But such considerations had little influence on the first missionaries in the selection of their field of labour. This seems to have been due mainly to the fact that this was the land of Sikhs — a people of fine physique, and unusually independent character; a people, moreover, who had already, in principle at least, discarded the old idolatry of Hinduism and broken, in some measure, the bonds of caste; and therefore might be considered to be in a favourable state to be influenced by the preaching of Christian missionaries.

After the pioneering work of Lowrie, missionaries from other Christian traditions also came to Panjab. The Church Missionary Society (Church of England) started its work at Simla and Kotegarh in 1840 and Amritsar in 1850; the American United Presbyterians at Sialkot in 1855; the Scottish Presbyterians at Chamba in 1863; the New Zealand Presbyterians at Jagathri in 1911; English Baptists in 1891 (later taken over by New Zealand Presbyterians in 1923); the Methodist Church in Southern Asia in Lahore in 1881. Other Christian traditions like the Salvation Army had missions at Lahore and Dhariwal. The Roman Catholics worked at Lahore, Amritsar and Jullunder Cantonment.

Thus by the end of the first quarter of the 20th century, evangelistic work by a variety of Christian denominations was going on all over the Panjab.

Panjabi culture

"Culture" in India has generally been accepted as synonymous with Hinduism. This is true in the case of most Christian scholars also. A.J. Appasamy's *The Gospel and India's Heritage* (London, 1942) is perhaps the best example of such a position, though almost the same stand is taken in a still older classic, namely *Rethinking Christianity in India* (Madras, 1938). This is also reflected in the choice of the various liturgical expressions through which different church traditions have made attempts to relate Christian worship to Indian culture. The problem with all these attempts is that they have failed to recognize the fact of both religious and cultural pluralism in India. For example, North West India (Panjab) is different from the rest of India in the same way as is North East India. Panjabi culture has been much influenced by the Sikh religious tradition, along with the liberal mystical traditions of Islam known as Sufi. It is a culture which is basically non-ritualistic and egalitarian in nature, unlike the classical Hindu traditions.

But it is also true that Panjabi culture, like other living cultural traditions of the world, has been changing according to the demands of time and context. In fact, Panjabi culture has gone through many such changes. Its history can be traced back to the pre-Christian era (around 2500-1500 BCE) with the flourishing, civilized culture of Mohenjodaro and Harappa, from where many ancient relics of sculpture, pottery, jewellery and fabric were excavated (1921-22), attesting to human occupation of these sites at that time. The archaeological investigations also revealed that these people were idol-worshippers, and images resembling Lord Siva were found. A number of other religious relics discovered indicate that this civilization was influenced by and related to later Hindu and other religious practices and thoughts, and in general to the culture of India of the generations to come.

The Aryans (who originally called themselves *arya*, which means "nobly born") were the first foreigners to come into Panjab, driving the original dwellers towards the central and southern parts of India. Originally pastoralists in the plains of Panjab, they became agriculturists with the passage of time. It was in Panjab that these Aryans also evolved the Vedic religion and literature.

After the Aryans other races followed into Panjab. In 326 BCE Alexander the Great came with his Greek army and settled for some time, leaving a Greek impression upon the land of Panjab. Later groups which came included the Tartars, the Moghuls and the Afghans — a fierce bloodthirsty race who for 700 years made the history of the Panjab a typical record of "the splendour and havoc of the East".

From 1801 to 1839 the Sikh ruler Maharajah Ranjit Singh, known as the Lion of Panjab, ruled. After his death the British took over Panjab in 1849 and ruled here until 1947. But even after independence, Panjabi culture has continued to change, both in India as well as in Pakistan. In India it has been influenced by the linguistic, religious and social traditions of the rest of India; in Pakistan it has come under the influence of Urdu language and Muslim religious traditions.

The coming of Christianity

By 1850 British rule was established in Panjab and at the same time Christianity had also started taking root in Panjab. We must remember that by this time there was, along with Hinduism and Islam, a third major religious force in Panjab, namely Sikhism. Sikhism as a religion has brought many changes in the overall life-style of the Panjabi people. At the time when it was founded by Guru Nanak (1469-1539), the religious and moral standards and traditions of Panjab had badly deteriorated. Guru Nanak himself described the conditions of his days in these words:

> The kings are butchers,
> Justice has taken wings and fled,
> the moon of truth is never seen to rise *(Var Majh)*.

Guru Nanak in his teachings condemned the social and cultural evils of Panjabi society, strongly criticizing those who oppressed women, the poor and the low castes. Similar teachings were propounded by the other nine Gurus. According to the Sikh scholar Gurbachan Singh Arshi, hatred towards the low castes greatly increased by the middle of the 19th century, and this tendency was being observed among the Sikhs also. Arshi points out another important factor which helped the Christian missionaries to establish themselves in Panjab. During the first half of the 19th century, he notes, the language of the Sikhs was Bhrij or Sadh-Bdhasa, not Panjabi. What is significant is that even though this was the period when Panjab was ruled by the Sikh ruler Maharajah Ranjit Singh, he did not try to introduce the language of their sacred Scripture and the language of the people as the official language.

In other words, when Christianity came to Panjab by the middle of the 19th century the social and cultural conditions of Panjab were not in good shape, which of course had a bearing on the future relationship of the gospel and culture in Panjab. Even so, Christianity encountered a well-established culture in Panjab and suffered many setbacks in the process. The encounter between, on the one side, the Christian gospel and, on the other side, Panjabi culture, along with Hinduism, Islam and in particular Sikhism, proved to be a stimulus for a cultural renaissance in the 19th century and also for the overall development of cultural nationalism in Panjab.

A number of factors were responsible for this cultural renaissance. First, thousands of low-caste people embraced Christianity; and this had a positive effect on Hinduism, Islam and Sikhism, bringing about a renewal and reawakening among the followers of these religions. A second factor was a new thrust in the area of the Panjabi language and literature, which served as a positive force for both Christianity and the Panjabi culture. A third factor was education, which helped to revive and increase the national spirit among the Panjabis and made them aware of the higher values of their culture. While other factors could be cited which enabled Christianity to play an effective role in relation to Panjabi culture and vice-versa, we will limit ourselves in the remainder of this booklet to these areas and the light they shed on an understanding of the functioning of the gospel in Panjab.

2. The Gospel at Work in Panjab

The movement of the Spirit

The basic task of Christian missionaries, as of the Christian church itself, is to proclaim the gospel of Christ and to win human beings to faith and obedience in him. This is precisely what Christian missionaries came to do in Panjab. But it is interesting to see that things in Panjab did not turn out in the way the missionaries had expected.

At the outset the missionaries were interested only in preaching the Christian gospel to the upper-caste people. Andrew Gordon, a pioneer missionary of the United Presbyterian Church of the USA, with more than thirty years of experience in missionary work, admitted in 1898 that,

> in concluding these remarks about my own evangelistic work in the last decades, I may say briefly that I began with my eye upon the large towns and cities, but have been led from them to the country villages. I began with the educated classes and people of good social position, but ended among the poor and the lowly.

The result of this approach on the part of the missionaries was that by 1885 — after more than 50 years of proclaiming the gospel — they had only 477 communicant members, many of whom were not Panjabi Christians. Indeed, the first person to be baptized in Ludhiana (in April 1837) was an upper-caste Bengali Hindu. But then after 1885 we see a rapid change, with numbers continuing to grow. It is important to understand this change. In the beginning it not only troubled the missionaries, but also shook Panjabi society as a whole. Through this, we believe, the movement of God's Spirit is revealed very clearly, and we see God's option for and his working among the poor, lowly and downtrodden. But this "Spirit movement", which church historians have labelled the "Christian Mass Movement", was at first not taken as a happy sign by Christian missionaries in Panjab.

There have been very few so-called upper-caste persons who accepted the gospel. The best example of these is the famous Sikh convert Sadhu Sundar Singh, whom the well-known missionary C.H. Loehlin described as "the Panjabi church's gift to world Christianity".

In reality the Panjabi church and Christian community comes from the Dalit background. In the "Holy Spirit Movement" among Panjabi Dalits, an early Panjabi Dalit Christian named Ditt played a major role. Indeed, J. Waskom Pickett, in his famous work on *Christian Mass Movements in India*, said that the real founder of the church in Sialkot was "not Gordon, but Ditt". Sialkot district was the first place where the United Presbyterian Church in the USA started its mission work in Panjab.

The scope and length of this booklet do not allow us to go into detail about the responses of Panjabis to the gospel; instead, we will narrate two stories here as examples of how this call came and who responded to it. These cases are of Ditt and Sadhu Sundar Singh respectively.

The story of Ditt

The work of United Presbyterian Church (U.P. Mission) began in August 1855 with the arrival of its first missionary Andrew Gordon in Sialkot, Panjab. We have already said that the number of Christians in Panjab increased by thousands beginning in the 1880s. The number of Christians belonging to all missions in Panjab numbered 3796 in 1881. By 1901 this had increased tenfold to 37,980; and by 1921 the number had gone up tenfold again to 375,031.

What was the reason behind this increasing number of Christians? The answer to this question lies in the story of Ditt, for which the source is the first missionary Andrew Gordon himself. Here only the main points of the story are given.

The story of Ditt began when a man named Nattu, a Hindu of the Jat caste (a Panjabi upper caste), was baptized on 17 November 1872 by the missionary J.S. Barr. Nattu was not only from a high caste, he was also the son of a *lambardar* (village head) and the legal heir to his father's property and position. The missionaries were very happy about his conversion, but they were soon disappointed when Nattu forfeited his right to be his father's heir. For the missionaries he proved a failure, "a weak brother". But this was far from the truth, for Nattu was to become an instrument in bringing into the Christian fold a person who would later became one of the main leaders responsible for the church and Christian community of Panjab. This man's name was Ditt.

Ditt came from a small village called Shahabdike, which was about 3 km. from the larger village of Mirali, and about 50 km. from Sialkot (which is now in Pakistan). He was born around 1843. Gordon introduces him in these words: "... a man of the low and much despised *chura* tribe..., a dark man, lame of one leg, quiet and modest in his manners, with sincerity and earnestness, well expressed in his face, and at that time about thirty years of age". By profession Ditt was a dealer of hides. He came in contact with Nattu, who taught him about Jesus Christ; and in June 1873 Nattu took him to Sialkot for baptism.

The missionary in Sialkot, S. Martin, was hesitant to accept Ditt for baptism. After all, his Christian faith was based on the teachings of the "weak brother" Nattu. At the same time, Ditt's knowledge of Christianity was quite sound, and he appeared to Martin to be an honest person. In any case when Martin suggested that they delay his baptism, Ditt was not willing. In the words of Gordon: "Mr Martin finally decided to baptize Ditt, not because he saw his way decidedly clear to do so, but rather because he could see no scriptural ground for refusing."

Martin faced another problem immediately after the baptism, when Ditt asked permission to go back to his village instead of staying in a protected mission compound. This was something new for Martin. The practice was that a new convert stayed with the missionary for more instruction and protection. Martin was worried about how this poor illiterate man would deal with the opposition he would inevitably face in his village. In the end, however, Ditt returned to Shahabdike and this decision on his part proved to be the starting point for a Christian movement among the ex-*churas* (Dalits) of Panjab.

On reaching home, Ditt did face bitter opposition from his own relatives. One of his fellow villagers rebuked him by saying: "Oho! You have become a *Sahib*" [gentleman]. Others said: "You have become a *be-i-man*" [one without religion]. His own sister-in-law said: "Alas, my brother, you have changed your religion without even asking our counsel; our relationship with you is over. Henceforth you shall neither eat, drink, nor in any way associate with us. One of your legs is broken already, so may it be with the other."

But Ditt did not care about any opposition. Instead he witnessed his new faith in Christ openly and boldly, both to his family members and others. The result was amazing. Three months after his baptism in August 1873, he had the privilege of taking his wife, his daughter and two neighbours to Sialkot for baptism. He had to walk for 50 km. for the sole purpose of introducing his family and friends to the missionaries. Fully satisfied by his examination, Martin baptized them.

Ditt's work of buying and selling hides took him to many different villages. Wherever he went on business, he preached about Christ also. In the eleven years after his baptism, he brought more than five hundred people from his caste to the Christian faith. By 1900 half the people of his community had accepted Christ, and by 1915 almost all the Dalits known as *churas* of Sialkot district had become Christians.

The missionaries, it seemed, were not interested in the Dalits becoming Christians. Some in fact were genuinely troubled about the way God's Spirit was working. In a letter to his mission board in March 1884 one missionary, J.C.R. Ewing, described this trend of poor, low castes becoming Christians as "raking in rubbish into the church". Other missionaries even hesitated to mention these converts' social background in their reports. Still others described them as "common villagers" or "illiterate menials".

But the conversions continued and today in Panjab there are about 250,000 Christians on the Indian side, of which 99 percent come from the Dalit background. The majority of Panjabi Christians are on the Pakistan side, and they share the same background.

However, this historical response of the early missionaries to the conversion of the Dalits has had a lasting negative effect on Panjabi Christianity; and even today Panjabi Christians ignore or are afraid to talk about the past, which would reveal their low social background.

Although at a later stage the missionaries accepted this trend as an integral part of their mission work, for a long time they were not fully convinced. For the sake of a few converts from the so-called privileged castes, they were forced to maintain double standards in the church.

The problem surfaced most visibly in worship services and around the communion table, which were, after all, the only occasions on which the two groups of Christians could meet. According to Mark Juergensmeyer, in his *Religion as Social Vision* (1982), they sought to resolve this problem in two ways —

> by establishing worship services for those who spoke English and those who spoke only Panjabi, which *de facto* eliminated the lower castes from English-speaking services; or, failing this, by ensuring that upper-caste converts would sit at the front of the church so that they would use the communion implements first, before they become polluted by the Christians of lower castes (p.188).

During my stay in the city of Jullunder in the early 1970s, I was told that the system of reserving front benches for the privileged ones had been abolished only a few years earlier.

Besides these administrative methods to deal with the problem in church services, the missionaries also used another method: that of establishing "mission compounds" in the towns, "Christian colonies" in cities and "Christian villages" for the rural people. These can still be found today; for example, there is a Christian village called Santokh Majra, established in 1870, near Karnal, and a mission compound in Jullunder.

Establishing these separate places for Panjabi Christians helped to create a very distinctive Christian culture and also projected an image which reflected the *chura* culture, the culture of the sweeper or lower class, although there were among them a few who had belonged to other castes.

The story of Sadhu Sundar Singh

Sadhu Sundar Singh was a Christian convert from a Sikh background. *Sadhu* means "holy" or "saint" or "ascetic"; and this title was used for a non-formal order of wandering holy men belonging to different religious faiths. Since Sundar Singh adopted this style of life after becoming a Christian, he was popularly known by others as "Sadhu".

Sundar Singh was born on 3 September 1889 in the village of Rampur, which is about 15 km. from Ludhiana in Panjab. His father, Sardar Sher Singh, was a rich farmer; and the family practised the Sikh religion. Sundar Singh's life as a Christian began on 3 September 1903, the day of his baptism, and he witnessed to his Christian faith vigorously until 18 April 1929, when he was last seen before undertaking a missionary journey to Tibet. Sadhu Sundar Singh's conversion and life story offer another example of the "Spirit movement".

Sadhu Sundar Singh's mother was a very religious woman; and it was she who had the greatest influence on him throughout his life. She was very fond of him and was his guide for his religious life. She used to say to him, "You must not be superficial and worldly like your brothers... You must seek peace of the soul and love religion, and one day you will become a holy Sadhu." These words of his mother continued to echo deeply in his soul throughout his life.

When Sadhu was fourteen years old, his mother died, and that led to a religious crisis in his young life. After that he began to study the various Sikh and Hindu scriptures with greater zeal. His guru (religious teacher) told his father that his son would "either become a fool or a great man". He even learned the practice of Yoga under the guidance of a Hindu *sannyasi* (ascetic). But all these efforts of Sundar Singh in search of peace came to naught.

He was then sent to Ludhiana to study in a mission school. There he was given the New Testament as a textbook, but he refused to read it, having been warned by others not to study the Bible. He developed a complete hatred towards Christianity. He even burned the Bible. When he saw the missionaries coming to preach the gospel, he was in the habit of abusing them. All these things he did even against the advice of his father. But his answer was: "The religion of the West is false; we must annihilate it."

Then came the great day of decision, 16 December 1904. On that day Sundar Singh felt a great inner pain, restlessness and unhappiness. Nothing could give him peace. He went to his father on the evening of 17 December and told him he had come to say good-bye, because before the next morning he would die. He said that no religion or money or comfort was of any help in giving him peace. His intention was to commit suicide by putting himself on the railway lines in front of a train which used to pass by his village at five o'clock in the morning.

So on 18 December, he rose at three o'clock and took a cold ceremonial bath according to the Hindu and Sikh custom. Then he prayed, "O God — if there be God — show me the right way and I will become a Sadhu; otherwise, I will kill myself." He continued to pray for a long time until there came an answer to his prayer.

Suddenly about 4:30 in the morning a great shining light appeared in his small room. At first he did not understand what this light was, so he continued to pray. But then he saw the figure of a human being in the shining light. First he thought this human figure was of Buddha or Krishna or some other divinity to whom he was praying. He was about to prostrate himself in front of this apparition when to his amazement he heard these words from the mouth of the human figure addressing him: "*Tu mujhe kyun satata hai? Dekh main ne tere liye apni jan salib par di*" ("Why do you persecute me? I gave my life for you upon the cross.") At the moment he heard these divine words, Sundar Singh recognized Jesus, who was looking at him with love, and then the thought came to him: "Jesus Christ is not dead. He is alive; and this is he himself." He fell at his feet and worshipped him. In an instant Sundar Singh felt his whole being changed, and he was filled with divine life, peace and joy in his inner soul. He rose from his feet. By that time Christ had disappeared, but this vision proved to be the turning point of Sundar Singh's life.

After this he dedicated his whole life to Christ and to the work of preaching the gospel. But he was sent away from his house. His family not only rejected him, but even tried to poison him; however, God saved him. He was formally baptized on 3 September 1905 in Simla, and on the next day he left on his mission. Many biographies of him have been written, both by Indian and foreign writers. One of the best known is *The Gospel of Sadhu Sundar Singh* by Friedrich Heiler (1989), which gives a first-hand description of Sadhu Sundar Singh's conversion in his own words (pp.41-44).

Many Indian Christian scholars have written wonderful books with original ideas regarding indigenous or contextual Christianity and how the Christian religion must take root in the Indian soil. But Sadhu Sundar Singh was one who lived the indigenous Christianity as its true follower. It was not a matter of intellectual exercise for him; it was in fact part of his real life. Some have even compared him with St Paul and St Augustine, who were proud of being Jewish and Christian and Roman and Christian respectively. The same is true about Sadhu Sundar Singh.

Many Indians have rejected the Christian faith because it has generally not taken root in the soil of our country. Sadhu Sundar Singh said that Indians do need the Water of Life, but not in the European cup. Among practical steps in contextualizing Christianity, Sadhuji said that Christians should sit down on the floor in the church. They should take off their shoes instead of their turbans. They should use Indian music, and the sermon should be replaced by an informal address.

Sadhu Sundar Singh always wore the saffron robe and turban, even during his travels in the West. Not only his external appearance, but the impression left by his whole personality was such that it was said about him that he looked "as if he had stepped straight out from the pages of the Bible". Once when he was visiting a town in a Western country he went and knocked at the door of a house. A servant came to the door and after opening it, she immediately rushed back inside, leaving Sadhu Sundar Singh standing at the door. She told her mistress, "There's someone who wants to see you, Ma'am. I can't make anything of his name. But he looks as if he might be Jesus Christ." A true *chela* (disciple) of a true Guru (teacher), Sadhu Sundar Singh became the image of his Guru. How many disciples of Jesus Christ can make the same claim?

The Spirit movement among other faiths

The acceptance of the gospel by the Dalits shook the Hindus, Muslims and Sikhs of Panjab when they saw thousands of these people whom they had ignored becoming Christians. They felt a sense of responsibility for creating this situation, and that forced them to examine themselves, evaluate and rethink, which brought a renaissance among the followers of these religions. Here we can give only a brief description of this renaissance, which began because of the presence of the gospel. This was another form of "Spirit movement", which introduced a positive change in the life of the followers of other faiths.

A number of Hindu organizations came into existence as a result of this new trend. For example, in 1872 the first temple of the Brahmo Samaj was started in Lahore. The Arya Samaj began in Lahore in 1878 to check the influence of

Christianity. According to Gurbachan Singh Mahita, "the purposes of this movement were to study Vedas, to condemn idol worship, to stress simple living, to oppose Western influences, to oppose casteism and through Sudhi to bring back those people to the Hindu fold who have become Christians". In addition to these organizations, in 1887 the Dev Samaj and in 1889 the Sanaatan Dharam Shaba were also established in Panjab to counter the Christian missionary movement.

The gospel work among the Dalits also awakened the Muslims. One important result was the establishment in 1889 of the famous Ahmadiyah movement, founded by Mirza Ghulam Ahmed (1839-1903) in Quadian Gurdaspur, Panjab. The rise of the movement is explained by Wilfred Cantwell Smith "as a protest against Christianity and the success of Christian proselytization; a protest also against Sir Sayyid Ahmed's rationalism and Westernization, and at the same time a protest against the decadence of the prevailing Islam".

Among the Sikhs, a number of reform movements came into existence as reaction against Christian mission work. For example, Baba Dayal Singh (1773-1855) started Nirankari Lahir to counter the preaching of Christianity, to weed out the many social evils which had arisen within the Sikh community and to stress the worship of Nirankar. Another major movement to reform Sikh society was Namdari or Kuka Lahir, launched by Baba Balak Singh (1799-1862) and Baba Ram Singh.

But the most important of the movements that began among the Sikhs during the 19th century was the Singh Sabha movement, which grew out of an incident in which four Sikh students — Aiva Singh, Alan Singh, Sadhu Singh and Santokh Singh — who were studying in a mission school in Amritsar were about to be baptized as Christians in 1873. Their baptisms were stopped; and in the same year the first meeting of the Sahba was held in Amritsar. The main purpose of this movement was to create an awakening in both Sikh religious and social life through education among the Sikhs.

3. Encounter and Responses

It is a widely recognized fact that language is one of the most important aspects of any culture. Language is not only a medium of communication among people, but it is actually the vehicle for expression of the culture as a whole. Language also helps in distinguishing different human cultures. Therefore, in this chapter we shall consider the Panjabi language and literature, which will assist us further in understanding the relationship of the gospel and Panjabi culture since the time of the arrival of Christianity on the soil of Panjab. We shall look at three facets of this relationship: the missionaries' response, the Panjabi Christians' response, and the response of Panjabi creative writers.

Missionaries' response

Panjabi is the official language of the Panjab state. It is written in one of the oldest scripts of India, the present name of which is Gurmukhi — from *gur* (teacher) and *mukh* (mouth); hence "from the mouth of the Guru, or teacher".

The Sikh Gurus, the ten great teachers of the Sikh religion, popularized Gurmukhi script; and the Sikh scripture, known in Panjabi as the Guru Granth Sahib, was written in this script. From this association with the Sikh Gurus, this script took the name Gurmukhi.

About the Panjabi language and script, the Presbyterian missionary E.P. Newton wrote in the introduction to his *Panjabi Grammar* (Ludhiana, 1898):

> The language which is spoken with some variation throughout the Panjab, and hence called Panjabi, is usually written in what is known as the Gurmukhi character... The arrangement of letters here is more systematic than that of the English alphabet.

In many countries the history of the Christian church, the translation of the Bible and the development of the language and literature have been closely inter-related. This is certainly true of the Panjab. Within twelve months of his arrival in Ludhiana, John Newton not only began a new translation of the New Testament into Panjabi (as an earlier translation made in 1815 by the Serampore missionaries in Bengal was of little practical use), but also established a printing press there. Newton's translation of Matthew's gospel came out in 1840. This was followed by John's gospel in 1841. In 1868 he published the whole New Testament in Panjabi.

However, Newton's contribution to the development of the Panjabi language was not limited to his translation of the New Testament. Missionaries coming to the Panjab needed books in order to learn the language. So Newton prepared the first comprehensive *Grammar of the Panjabi Language*, published in 1851, as well as the first *Vocabulary Book*, published in 1854, which was 438 pages long. He and Levi Janvier, his cousin and fellow Presbyterian missionary, who had already begun (but never finished) a translation of the Old Testament into Panjabi, completed the first dictionary of the Panjabi language in 1854 after twelve years of work.

Newton also encouraged and trained local authors and translators. One of these was Sharda Ram Philori, who was encouraged by Newton to write his best book, *Panjabi Bat Cheet*, which means "Panjabi conversation". Sharda Ram Philori's other notable prose writing in Panjabi is the description of the Sikh kingdom (1866). His first work received an award from the government, and his writings are today considered the best examples of the prose of his time.

Levi Janvier published his translation of the book of Genesis and the first 20 chapters of Exodus in 1851. The Ludhiana Mission Press published a number of works in Panjabi. Those in my collection include *Dharam Marg* (The Way of Religion) (1864), *Bible Dian Muytan Ate Kananian* (Pictures and Stories of the Bible) (1878), *Enjilsar* (Summary of the Gospel) (1880), and *Pilgrim's Progress*.

Another early Presbyterian missionary whose contribution is especially worth noting is John Newton's son Edward Payson Newton, who served as chairman of the revision committee appointed in 1889 to produce a new Panjabi translation of the New Testament. This was published in 1900. No further translation work was done on the Old

Testament for many years. E.P. Newton also produced a Panjabi grammar, published in 1898. In the introduction he showed that the Gurmukhi script is one of the oldest scripts in India. About the characters of this script he wrote:

> Of the entire number (35) no less than twenty-one can, though they have undergone some change, be distinctly recognized in the ancient inscriptions; six at least are traceable to the 10th century of our era; three to the 5th century and twelve to the 3rd century before Christ.

In 1947 India and Pakistan became independent countries and the Panjab was partitioned between them. Soon afterwards a translation committee was formed in the Indian Panjab to translate the Old Testament into Panjabi. The major responsibility for this work fell upon C.H. Loehlin, a Presbyterian missionary, and Sundar Singh of the United Church of North India. This translation was completed in 1959 and published along with the New Testament. So for the first time we had the whole Panjabi Bible in the Gurmukhi script. This translation of the Bible, which can be found in almost all major libraries in Panjab, is one of the greatest gifts of the missionaries not only to the Panjabi church and people, but also to Panjabi language, literature and culture.

Work on the translation of the Panjabi Bible has continued into our time also. After Loehlin's work was completed in 1959, the Bible Society of India for the first time appointed a Panjabi translator, in the person of the author of this booklet, in February 1971, along with a five-member committee to supervise work on a new translation of the Bible in the Panjabi language. The translation of the New Testament was completed in 1975 and the Old Testament in 1980. The Bible Society of India published the new complete Panjabi Bible; and it was officially launched by the former president of India, Giani Zail Singh, on 2 March 1985.

Currently editorial work on the new Panjabi translation is going on. I am serving as the editor, along with a small team of Panjabi Christian scholars. In this work, the new developments and changes which have taken place in the cultural life and language of Panjab since the partition in 1947 are being taken into account.

Panjabi Christians' response

The gospel in fact took root in Panjabi soil and was incarnated in Panjabi culture through the writings of Panjabi Christians. The efforts of these Panjabi Christians can be considered on the one hand as their response to the gospel and on the other hand as a contribution to Panjabi culture and language. Here we shall look briefly at five examples of such early writings in Panjabi.

1. *Mangalsamachar*, by Padri Daud Singh (1873)

Padri Daud Singh was the first Sikh convert of the Church Missionary Society. He was baptized in Kanpur by W.H. Perkins. Padri Daud Singh was transferred to Amritsar in 1852 and was ordained in 1854. He died in January 1882 at Clarkabad (Pakistan), where he was a pastor at the time.

Padri Daud Singh was perhaps the first Panjabi Christian poet. One of his works, only a part of which has survived, was a translation of the gospel according to St Matthew into Panjabi, under the title *Mangalsamachar*. In this translation he used the different forms of Panjabi *candu-bandhi* (verses) known as *doha, kabit, chobola*, etc. As is well-known, translation work is especially difficult in the case of poetry, since the translator has to overcome the twofold challenge of faithfully rendering the original text while following the principles of a particular form of poetry. Padri Daud Singh successfully maintained a balance between these two requirements.

Equally noteworthy is the theological contribution he made through the use of different expressions and phrases from his own Panjabi cultural background. He has recounted very beautifully and accurately the encounter of Joseph with an angel and his vision about the birth of Jesus. He narrated this in a *kabit*, in which he uses the expression *Paramatma* for the Holy Spirit and *Isa* for God. Both these terms are used in the hymns of Guru Nanak, the first with the meaning "the supreme or universal soul", the second with the meaning "Lord". In one of Padri Daud Singh's *doha*, he inserts the voice from heaven which said at the time of Jesus' baptism, "This is my beloved Son, with whom I am well pleased". Padri Sahib has translated this as:

> *Dekho Ik rav gagan se nikasa eh kahat,*
> *Yih mere priya putr hai jis se mai mudat.*
> (See, a voice came from above in heaven,
> This is my beloved Son, with whom I am happy.)

2. *Sat Swami Nihakalank Autar Prabhu Jisu Masih Da Jas Dharam Pustak Anusar*, by Tahil Singh (1900)

Unfortunately, no other biographical information is available regarding Tahil Singh than what he has left for us in this work entitled "The story of Jesus Christ in Panjabi Verse". This was published by the Panjab Religious Book Society, Anarkali, Lahore, in 1900. It includes 126 pages of text (in addition to a four-page list of other books published by the same society). In keeping with the tradition of his time, Tahil Singh left the stamp of his name as the last line of his work, which reads as follows:

> *Tahil Singh Kirapa tujh upar tainu*
> *bhi apane pas bulaaio.*
> (Tahil Singh, you have received his grace,
> He will call you to himself.)

He also indicates in one of his *doha* that he is a serious researcher of the Scripture *(khoj anjil)*.

As was typical of his time, Tahil Singh has used various kinds of *cand* (verses) to praise his "Sat Swami Nihakalank autar Prabhu Jesu Masih" — *dohara, kundalila, savaiya, korara, kabit, chopai* and *mithara*. The term *cand* has its roots in the Sanskrit *candas* — "to praise". Thus the *candabandhi* form of Panjabi poetry is appropriate to such a work.

While following the Panjabi *kavi-parampara* (poetic tradition) of the late 19th century, Tahil Singh uses a metrical form of poetry.

Theologically, the work of Tahil Singh is highly original, and certainly represents one of the pioneering attempts at an indigenous local expression of theology, particularly of Panjabi Christology. This is brought out in the titles which Tahil Singh uses for Jesus Christ. These titles include *Sat* (truth), *Swami* (Lord), *Nihakalank* (sinless one), *Autar* (taking the form of human), *Prabhu* (Lord), *Satigur* (true teacher), *Raja* (king), *Antarajami* (one who knows the inner side of a being), *Guru* (teacher) and *Sardar* (chief). Tahil Singh did not use these titles simply for the sake of variety; each one reveals his feelings and convictions. For example, after receiving the message from the angel about the birth of Jesus, he expresses what happened to Joseph, in a *kundalia cand* which includes the line:

> *Yusuf ko nisacha bhaia,*
> *Iha satigur ki mani.*
> (Joseph believed that she [Mary]
> is the mother of a True Teacher.)

Tahil Singh's use of indigenous titles for Jesus is very natural. About Jesus' meeting a sick person who had been suffering for 38 years, Tahil Singh says in a *doha*:

> *Antarajami hai parbhu ik mila bimar bhata*
> *Baras athathi se para ohada koi na jor chala.*
> (The Lord knows the inner side of a person. He met a sick person, who for 38 years was there, but could do nothing.)

A line from a *kabit* shows how Tahil Singh introduces the doctrine of ransom (*jamni*):

> *Jag jamni jahan se salib*
> *pai uthaio.*
> (He paid the ransom for the world on the cross.)

Tahil Singh introduces the doctrine of the incarnation (*autar*) of Jesus through the mouth of the angel as he brought the message to the shepherds. A line from his *savaia*:

Isa autar bhaio aj rat mai,
Vekh alo sahir mai tum jaai.
(Today at night Jesus has taken incarnation;
you go to the city to see it.)

But Tahil believed that the *autar* Jesus was a fully human being, not only a shadow as understood in Indian religious tradition. This is clear from his following *doha*:

Pahila adam mot de dusara jindagi de.
Parabhu adam mai ai kar pure kam kare.
(The first man gives death, the second gives life. By becoming human, the Lord completes all the works.)

By using the Panjabi religious thought form, Tahil Singh in one of his *chopai* gives the meaning of the concept of new birth or second birth about which Jesus spoke to Nicodemus:

Ruh bigare jab marad ki bure karam tab hon.
Sati sangar mil bhata ho bhale karam pher hon.
(When the mind of a person gets dirty, then he becomes a source of evil deeds. If he gets back into a true fellowship, he again becomes a source of good deeds.)

In this *chopai* the concept of *sati sangat* (true fellowship) is added: the idea of new birth is attuned to the Panjabi ethos through the concept of *sati sangat*.

Tahil Singh used the *korara* form to deal with the final judgment. He directly addresses those who call themselves Christians, but do not follow the teachings of Christ. Like a real *korara* (whip), he uses the appropriate form of Panjabi poetry:

Isa akhe suno Isaio Kahun mai Ik kahani
Roj kiamat pucunga tusa suni kalam rabani.
Nanga bhukha mai piasa tusan nahin pataia pani.
Mera hukam na mana tum nai samajhi jhuth kahani.
(Jesus says, "O Christians, hear, I will tell you a story.
At the time of judgment, I will ask you if you heard the gospel.
I was hungry, I was thirsty, but you did not give me water.
You did not believe in my teaching, because you took this story of truth as false.)

In this work Tahil Singh uses many other phrases and expressions which have deep theological meanings but are at the same time deeply rooted in the Panjabi soil, among them *sangat* (fellowship), *bhagat* (devotee), *kirapa* (mercy), *balidan* (sacrifice), *aradas* (prayer).

3. *Panjabi Zabur* (Panjabi Psalms), by Imam-ul-Din Shahbaz

Imam-ul-Din Shahbaz, one of the early Panjabi Christians, in fact made a contribution to the entire Indian church through his work on *Zabur* (Psalms). Shahbaz was born in Zaffarwal (now in Pakistan). He was baptized in the Church Missionary Society's mission in Amritsar, but in July 1880 he was transferred to the Gurdaspur district to work with the United Presbyterian Church.

While working as an evangelist in the area of Gurdaspur, Shahbaz's base was Sialkot (now in Pakistan). It was here during the 1880s that he worked on the book of Psalms and adapted and made a metrical Panjabi version, which is perhaps the only case in which all 150 Psalms are available in poetic and singable form in an Indian language. All of the Psalms have been adapted to local Panjabi tunes. The first complete edition to be published in the Persian script, which appeared in 1905, was followed by others in 1916, 1925 and 1936. In the Roman script the complete edition was first published in 1908. In 1930 and 1933 selections were published in the Gurmukhi script.

As with the earlier works, we shall limit our comments here to the contents. One way to look at this is to begin with the sub-headings provided by Padri Shahbaz at the beginning of each *Zabur*. These headings help to convey the idea or conviction Shahbaz had in mind while working on that *Zabur*. For example, *Zabur* 31 (part one), is headed by *Masihi da Bharosa* (the trust of a Christian). What Shahbaz means by this heading is made clear right at the beginning of the *koras* (refrain):

Meri as hai tere ute ai yhuva
pak khuda.
(You are my hope, O Lord, Holy God.)

This *koras* is also the first line of verse 1 of Psalm 31. In the *koras* Shahbaz uses the term *pak* for "righteous", whereas in verse 1 he uses another term, *sachiai*, which recurs in verse 5, where it is used for the "faithfulness" of God, who is addressed as *sachiai de khuda*. Anybody who has gone through Panjabi religious literature, particularly the Adi Granth, the sacred scripture of the Sikh religion, will immediately recognize that *sat* (truth) or *sach* (true) is an attribute of God, in which, according to Shahbaz, a *Masihi* (Christian) is supposed to place his or her confidence and trust.

Padri Iman-ul-Din Shahbaz was not only a poet and a scholar, but he had a very critical eye, which is evident from his use of the words and phrases of Psalm 80 (part two). Here he could see the degraded conditions described in the content of this Psalm reflected in the church of the day. The original Hebrew title of this *Zabur* means a "testimony", perhaps written about the conditions of the people at the time when the Psalm was composed. But Shahbaz changed this title into *Kalisia di giri hoi halat* (the fallen condition of the church). He also makes a link between the historical background of the church *(Panjabi Kalisia)* with Israel's slavery in *Misar* (Egypt). After all, the Panjabi church had a similar background. In a way, it was even worse, because the majority of Panjabi Christians were still living more or less as bonded labourers (slavery), through the process of *sepi* (men's yearly contracted work with the landlord), which involved *goha cutana* (removing cow dung) and life in a *thathi* — the place outside the village, where low-caste people were obliged to live. As long as these expressions continue to be part of the reality of Panjabi Christians' lives, the words used by Shahbaz in the heading as well as in the text (vv.8,15) will remain relevant to the conditions of the church even today. He says:

Koras — *Asin dige han sanun Uthaiu,*
apana cheraha tun savnu vikhaiu...
8. Tu ik dakh di taihani Misaro le aya...
15. Ujari hai Oha dakh jangal de suran,
te Khande sab jangali os tak
(Refrain: We have fallen, raise us,
show us your face...
8. You brought a grapevine out of Egypt...
15. Wild boars trampled that grapevine down,
and all wild animals feed on it).

4. *Malaka Astar (Kissa)*, by Musa Khan (1924)

Kissa-Kavi parampara, the tradition of narrative poetry in Panjabi, came into being during the 19th century under the influence of the Persian tradition. This form was used to narrate long love stories. Musa Khan's *kissa Malaka Astar*, which is based on the biblical story of Esther, is part of this tradition. The fact that this Old Testament story has its setting in Persia may explain why Musa Khan used it as the basis of a narrative poem in a form coming from the Persian tradition. By the time he wrote this *kissa*, the *kissa* tradition in Panjabi was well established among the masses. Unfortunately, we do not have any biographical information about Musa Khan except what we learn from his *kissa*.

Musa Khan has brought out a number of points very clearly in the text of this *kissa*. One point which is made forcefully is that India was part of the biblical world, because India at the time of Esther was one of the 127 provinces of the kingdom of Persia (cf. Esth. 1:1). At the same time, the poet very powerfully describes the attitude of men towards women at the time of Esther. For example, the reason Queen Vashti had to suffer was not so much her refusal to come to the open court on show as it was the fear of the men that, by following her example, all other women would also become free and independent. So the royal advisors (all of them men, of course) persuaded the king to punish Vashti. Otherwise:

> *Baki rania bhi bigar jania je,*
> *Characha hovega ja baja sain,*
> *aki auratan hongi khanvda tou.*
> (Other queens will also go astray,
> when this news goes out,
> women in general will go out of order.)

If on the other hand Vashti is punished and the king removes her as queen and takes another woman in her place, all the other women will be more careful in future. Musa Khan expresses the negative feelings of men in these words:

> *Tan jo kan hovan sari timian nu,*
> *rahin marad'a di Vich raja sain.*
> (So that all women will learn a lesson,
> and they will go according to the wishes of men.)

But Musa Khan's main purpose in taking up the story of Esther is to encourage the readers to live for others and, if they have to die, to do so in the service of others. According to him, one should live for his or her *kom* (community). That is the only life worth living; otherwise, all life is worthless:

> *jekar kom de kam na asin tai,*
> *jano jidagi gai bekar beli.*
> *Vangu Asatar Kom te Karo sara*
> *tan man te dhan nasar beli.*
> (If we do not serve our community,
> O friend, our whole life has gone to waste.
> Like Esther [you] should sacrifice all body,
> mind and wealth for your community.)

5. *Dastan-I-Yusaf (kissa)*, by Jwahar Das (1933)

Kissa Dastan-I-Yusaf — or, as it is known among common people, *Yusuf da Kissa* — is the story of Joseph in Panjabi verse. This *kissa* by Jwahar Das was published by the Panjabi Religious Book Society, Anarkali, Lahore. Again, we do not have any information about the life of Jwahar Das. His *kissa* is the only witness which we have in order to discover his commitment.

The story of this *kissa* is taken from the Bible. Before it was published, another *kissa* was available under the title *Yusaf-Jalaikhan*, written by the Muslim poet Hafij Bara Khuradar. There are both differences and similarities between the story of *Yusaf-Jalaikhan* and the *Dastan-I-Yusaf* of Jwahar Das. It seems that Jwahar Das was acquainted with the work of Hafij Bara Khuradar; thus he makes the claim that the story of his *kissa* was true, because it is found in the word of God, while other *kisse* (he does not mention any by name) were based on stories which were not factual.

Jwahar Das considered the writing of his *kissa* a part of his Christian vocation. Thus he closes it with a personal testimony:

> *Jwahar Das hai banda tera nal lahu mul lita,*
> *tere hathon gisu piare parem piala pita.*
> (Jwahar Das is your servant, who has been bought with your blood, he has drunk from your hand, beloved Jesus, the cup of love.)

Panjabi creative writers' response

Evidence of how the gospel has taken root in Panjabi soil and touched Panjabi culture is also found in the creative writings of Panjabi writers belonging to other faiths, especially those from a Sikh background. Here we can offer only a few examples of this.

Waris Shah (1720-1795), a Muslim, was one of the famous Panjabi poets of the 18th century, who wrote a *kissa* entitled *Heer*. Heer is the main female character, whose lover is beaten and left half dead by his opponents. The poet shows Heer's deep concern for her lover by using the symbol of Christ's resurrection, even though Muslims of course do not believe in the resurrection:

> *Moaia Pia hai nal phirak Ranjau,*
> *Ise vangu mur pher jivavani han.*
> (Ranjha is dead now,
> Like Jesus [I will] bring him into life again.)

Another more recent poet, Pritam Singh Safir, a Sikh, says in one of his poems:

Plustino chal Ke,
Sadian dian vithan uton,
mere peeche aie.
(From Palestine, he came,
from the distance of ages he came after me.)

The work of several other Panjabi Sikh poets has been influenced by the symbols and message of the gospel. The well-known poet Harbhajan Singh, in a collection of poetry published under the title *Sarak de Safe Ute*, uses the symbol of the cross more than once. The well-known contemporary historian and poet Gopal Singh is perhaps the first Indian Panjabi poet to have written the whole life of Jesus Christ in English, by using the form of free verse under the title "The Man Who Never Died". The opening stanza and last few verses of this long poem give a sample of it and form an appropriate conclusion to this chapter:

This is the story of the Man
Who never died:
and Who proclaimed
that he who's born
must be re-born;
and he who's dead
must rise from the state of death...

And, so, when men thought,
all was over with Him,

He rose from the dead,

like lightning, with his garments, white
as snow, but appearing as if He were
a flame of fire.

Men around were struck with terror

But he said unto those that believe
that nothing dies in the realm of God —

neither seed, nor drop, nor dust, nor man.

Only the past dies or the present,
but the future lives for ever.

And, I'm the future of man.

To me, being and non-being were always one,
I always was and never was.

4. The Continuing Challenge to Panjabi Christians

The gospel on one side and the changing context of Panjabi culture on the other continue to challenge Panjabi Christians. The Panjabi Christian community is basically a Dalit church, coming historically from a background of those who were crushed and oppressed by the caste system. It belongs to the so-called *chura* community, considered not only to be the lowest part of Panjabi society but in fact to be outside the pale of human society.

Because according to the caste system these people are "out-caste", considered as untouchable and even non-human beings, the following words of St Paul, addressed to the Christians of Corinth, are especially appropriate when applied to Panjabi Christians:

> Consider your own call, brothers and sisters: not many of you were wise by human standards, not many were powerful, not many were of noble birth. But God chose what is foolish in the world to shame the wise; God chose what is weak in the world to shame the strong; God chose what is low and despised in the world, things that are not, to reduce to nothing things that are, so that no one might boast in the presence of God. He is the source of your life in Christ Jesus, who became for us wisdom from God, and righteousness and sanctification and redemption (1 Cor. 1:26-30).

While these words of St Paul are true in the case of Panjabi Christians, as a community they still have to taste the fuller redemptive aspects of the gospel. This is where they are faced with their first major ongoing challenge. The future mission task of the church has to be to bring complete salvation to these Christians as a community. Even though most of them come from families which have been Christian for three or four generations, their life as a whole — which includes social, economic and political as well as religious life — is the same as where they first started. Basically this is because they have not been preached the whole gospel, which can change one's whole life. They have been fed on "half salvation", which aims only to "show them the way to heaven". In other words, the focus is on individual piety. This has only provided an escape route for their psychological self, rather than bringing any real change in their life, temporally as well as spiritually.

Second, the church in Panjab, as well as in India as a whole, has to work out a new mission strategy, based upon the newly discovered social and religious composition of the Indian people. Until now, the various missionary movements and churches have based their mission programmes on the myth that India has a majority of people (about 85 percent) who are Hindus and that all of them are followers of the classical Brahminical religious traditions. But as the Mandal Commission Report on the Backward Classes of the government of India (1980) made clear, the truth is more complex than this. According to its findings, the composition of the Indian population is as follows:

— Dalits and indigenous communities: 22.56%
— Non-Hindu religious communities (Muslims, Christians and others): 16.16%
— Forward and Upper Caste Hindus: 17.58%
— Other Backward Classes (Hindu OBC): 43.70%

Up to this point our mission, as well as our theology, has been based upon the fewer than 18 percent of the Indian population (which include 5.5 percent Brahmins) who are the real followers of classical Hinduism. Today we have to reverse our base from this minority and turn the attention in our church programmes to the 82.42 percent of the people of India which includes Dalits, indigenous peoples, religious minorities and other backward classes.

This needs a bigger and bolder commitment to our mission task. This challenge is especially pertinent for Panjabi Christians, who share their cultural and social roots with this vast majority of the population. This of course also has important impliciations for the global Christian community, challenging it to change its view of the mission needs of India and the Panjab.

Finally, Panjabi Christians need to increase the vigour with which they continue to address the task of relating their Christian faith and their commitment to the gospel to Panjabi culture.

Selected Bibliography

Archer, John Clark, *The Sikhs in Relation to Hindus, Moslems, Christians and Ahmadiyya: A Study in Comparative Religion*, Princeton, 1941.

Arshi, Gurcharan Singh, *Panjabi Bhasha Te Sahit Nu Isai Missionaries di dan* (in Panjabi), Patiala, 1987.

Firth, Cyril Bruce, *An Introduction to Indian Church History*, Madras, 1981.

Gordon, Andrew, *Our Indian Mission, 1855-1885*, Philadelphia, 1888.

Heiler, Friedrich, *The Gospel of Sadhu Sundar Singh* (abridged translation by Olive Wyon), Delhi, 1989 (reprint).

Juergensmeyer, Mark, *Religion as Social Vision: The Movement against Untouchability in the 20th-Century Punjab*, Berkeley, 1982.

Mahita, Gurbachan Singh, *Dr Vir Singh di Kavita* (in Panjabi), Patiala, 1972.

Newton, John, *Historical Sketches of the Indian Missions of the Presbyterian Church in the United States of America*, Allahabad, 1886.

Picket, J. Waskom, *Christian Mass Movements in India*, New York, 1933.

Singh, Gandha, ed., *The Singh Sabha and Other Socio-Religious Movements in the Punjab, 1850-1925*, Patiala, 1984.

Streeter, B.H. and A.J. Appasamy, *The Sadhu: A Study in Mysticism and Practical Religions*, Delhi, 1987 (reprint).

Webster, John C.B., *The Christian Community and Change in the Nineteenth-Century North India*, Delhi, 1976.